C000286028

FAREWELL TO UPTON PARK

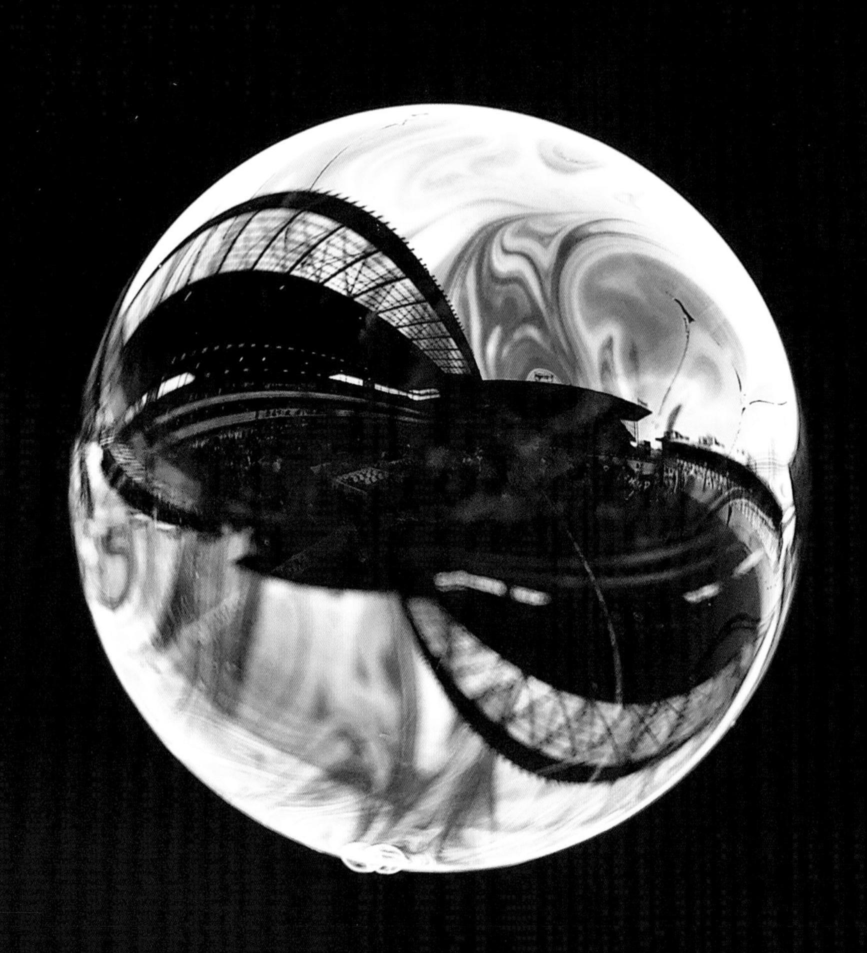

FAREWELL TO UPTON PARK

THE OFFICIAL CELEBRATION OF WEST HAM'S HOME 1904–2016

Andy Hooper & Lee Clayton

hamlyn

Andy Hooper is five times winner of Sports Photographer of the Year and winner of Royal Photographer of the Year and Football Photographer of the Year. He is the chief sports photographer for the *Daily Mail*, *Mail on Sunday* and *MailOnline*. He has been photographing West Ham for 25 years and this is his second book.

Lee Clayton is Group Head of Sport for the *Daily Mail*, *Mail on Sunday* and *MailOnline*. The *Mail* has been named Sports Newspaper of the Year for the last three years, voted for by the Sports Journalist Association, and Sports Team of the Year at the Press Awards. Lee is a West Ham season ticket holder and lives in London with his partner Kate and two daughters Molly and Olive.

For the supporters, who make West Ham so special

An Hachette UK Company
www.hachette.co.uk

First published in Great Britain in 2016 by Hamlyn, a division of
Octopus Publishing Group Ltd
Carmelite House
50 Victoria Embankment
London EC4Y 0DZ
www.octopusbooks.co.uk

ISBN 978 0 60063 4614

A CIP catalogue record for this book is available from the British Library.

Printed and bound in Italy

10 9 8 7 6 5 4 3 2 1

Editorial Director Trevor Davies
Creative Director Jonathan Christie
Designer Jeremy Tilston
Senior Editor Pauline Bache
Picture Research Manager Giulia Hetherington
Senior Production Manager Peter Hunt

CONTENTS

PLEASE
KEEP OFF
THE GRASS

THE WEST HAM FAMILY

SIR TREVOR BROOKING

I lived in Barking, just over two miles away from the stadium, until I was 16, and so my dad would drive in along the Barking Road, past Newham Town Hall and towards the junction of Green Street, by The Boleyn Tavern. Where the statue of West Ham's World Cup winners has stood in recent years was once public toilets. We'd take a left there and look for a parking space in one of the side roads. Some local lads used to ask for 20d to look after the car, so my dad – known as Harry – would pay them half upfront and the rest when we got back. This was around 1957–8. I signed for the Club in 1965, so more than 50 years ago and, though I moved out to Essex, I have been taking a similar journey for a long time.

As a supporter, I used to stand on the North Bank. I'd take a stool to stand on, and in those days children were passed down to the front, where their families would collect them after the game. I remember the Chicken Run, to our left, rocking as the fans swayed – it looked as though it might collapse. The fans there were within touching distance of the pitch. In later years when I took a corner in front of them, there was only enough room for two paces. They'd share a few choice words if you weren't having the best game.

I love West Ham. I spent my entire playing career at the Club, including three seasons as a player in the old Second Division. I'm not sure that would happen in the modern game, when the difference in wages is more significant and clubs who are relegated want to sell their best players to pay for the loss of top-flight status.

I stayed at West Ham for a number of reasons. The season we were relegated, 1977–8, was my testimonial year. Around 25,000 had come to the game against an England XI, supporters had bought pontoon tickets in pubs and there was a gala dinner. I didn't think it would be right to leave after that.

Ron Greenwood was the England manager, my old West Ham manager, and he was happy to continue to pick me in the Second Division, providing I maintained my form. That helped, too.

The next season we had the makings of a good side and won the FA Cup against Arsenal in May 1980 to qualify for Europe. The following season we won promotion with a record points total (in the last season of two points for a win). That promotion season of 1981 we had the best defence I had ever played in front of – Phil Parkes, Ray Stewart, Alvin Martin, Billy Bonds and Frank Lampard. It allowed the creative, attacking players such as myself and Alan Devonshire to make our mark. It was a good season and we were a good team, with John Lyall as manager. We reached the League Cup Final, losing to Liverpool.

West Ham supporters during those times epitomize our fans; they stayed through thick and thin, mostly thin. It created a West Ham family; a mixture of the players, the owners, the management and staff – and the fans. Why should I want to leave?

We all have our memories and our traditions. At the time when I joined the Club, in the summer of 1965, we had just won the FA Cup twice, in 1963 and 1964, and the European Cup Winners' Cup in May 1965, and the next year we saw Bobby Moore, Geoff Hurst and Martin Peters, our three players, lift the World Cup! It was an amazing time to be a West Ham supporter and a young West Ham player – our place was the place to be.

Now I look at the current team and the job Slaven Bilić has done in his first season as manager, creating an attractive side to watch, and I get a feeling of progression. West Ham could be dangerous, a team challenging for trophies again. I can understand the feeling of excitement. This is the best West Ham team for 20 years, and people want to come to see West Ham again, which is reflected in the surge in ticket sales at the Olympic Stadium.

If I have one wish for the new ground, it is for Billy Bonds to be recognized. There are tributes to Bobby Moore and myself, but Billy deserves to be up there as well. Billy was a gladiator, a warrior. However, if I stopped the sentence there, that would be an injustice. He wasn't just a swashbuckling leader, with his socks down and shin pads off – the famous Steve Bacon image of him with his face cut to pieces sums up that side of his game – but he could play, too.

My regret is that he never played for England; he should have done. In 1981, the year we came up with the record points total, he had been told by the England manager that he was to play against Argentina, alongside Alvin Martin, on the following Tuesday. We played Sheffield Wednesday on the Friday before that and needed to win to break the points record. A cross came in, Phil Parkes called it late – and when Phil came you got out of the way. Instead, Billy was sandwiched between Phil and the Wednesday striker Andy McCulloch. He knew immediately he had broken his ribs, but later told Phil he would rather break his ribs than see them score and rob us of the points record. He was that kind of person, even though it robbed him of his England chance.

My feeling was that if he had got into that team, it would have been hard to get him out. He was a man and a half, and when I look back on my West Ham career, he was our greatest player.

I'm sure you have your own memories – these are a few of mine from the place I have called 'home' for more than 50 years. Thank you for reading them.

FOREWORD

ARONESS KARREN BRADY

Γhe other day I watched a video
›f the first match back at the
3oleyn Ground after the 1966
Vorld Cup Final. It was against
Chelsea, traditionally among
West Ham's fiercest London
ıeighbours. Our three World
Cup-winning footballers –
hat-trick striker Geoff Hurst,
;oal-scorer Martin Peters
and, of course, captain Bobby
out alone to the centre circle
ere were fans in Panama hats, a
formed a guard of honour and
ıe wonder what it would have
porter inside the stadium that
ınd ownership as three home-
hared with the country weeks

am supporters have memories
team at the Boleyn Ground –
›bby gliding across the ground
.yall's 1986 team who finished
n. Or the delight in watching
:s of the Sixties, Seventies and
n adventures or the promotion-
an Pardew and Sam Allardyce
mention, too, Paolo Di Canio's
don, recently voted by our fans as the best goal ever scored at Upton Park. As well as Paolo and our World Cup winners, there have been players like the legendary Billy Bonds, Alvin Martin, Sir Trevor Brooking and, in our current team, the brilliant Dimitri Payet. Like our stadium in Green Street, they all belong to the rich heritage of this great Club. We should not forget the past, but it is time for fresh adventures.

Leaving the old stadium is a bit like moving out of the house where you were born: you take with you so many memories, it feels as if it is part of you, you're not sure you want to leave and there is a heaviness as you load up the last piece of furniture and head off to somewhere new. 'New' for us, for every West Ham fan, is the mightily impressive Olympic Stadium in Stratford and I am immensely proud of the role I have played in making that move possible.

This book is not the place to repeat the business reasons behind the transfer, or the justification to those who feel we have 'struck lucky'. I will, however, repeat that this is a great move – and a great deal – for West Ham, and none of us should feel the need to apologize for that. As we embark on this new adventure, with a manager and a team of whom we can all feel incredibly proud, I would like to say thank you for your patience and understanding. The support that has been shown in the sale of tickets is remarkable and it reveals West Ham to be a big Club. Now we need to stride out towards many more wonderful memories.

This project is something I have been excited about since the idea was originally mooted. None of us will forget Upton Park, but from this day onwards, the only way is up.

ERRATUM

The Publishers would like to apologise for an error on page 8, second paragraph, where the second sentence should read:

'At the time when I joined the Club, in the summer of 1965, we had just won the FA Cup in 1964 and the European Cup Winners' Cup in May 1965...'

The printed error was introduced at the editing stage.

INTRODUCTION

LEE CLAYTON

My granddad, Ron Goodacre, was a gentle but powerful man who, every Saturday, liked to watch men in tights (ITV *World of Sport* wrestling), munch on Conference pears with the skin removed, place a small bet on the horses and look out for West Ham. On a weekday, he would finish his shift in the docks and walk home to Cameron Street, Beckton, where we lived next door, in a two-bedroom terraced council house with an outside loo. I eagerly waited for him so we could talk football. He would bring the *Evening Standard* for me to study the sports pages, and one day in 1979 our favourite team made the front page: 'West Ham sign world record goalkeeper'. Phil Parkes was coming from Queen's Park Rangers to join our Second Division promotion drive.

West Ham and world records do not usually appear in the same sentence, but it was reported that six previous bids from the then Manchester United manager Dave Sexton had been rejected. Parkes really was coming to West Ham. I cut out the story to keep and it was the start of my love for newspapers. I always especially loved headlines about *my* team. That is what attracted me to my day job.

My scrapbook was bulging some years later when I was 16, and West Ham were in the first match on live television following a blackout because of the financial row between the clubs and the channels. The team won 1–0 at Charlton: Tony Cottee scored the winning goal and Frank McAvennie set him up with a lob over the advancing goalkeeper. The back-page headline in the *Daily Mirror* was 'Live from His Majesty' and it was accompanied with a black-and-white picture. McAvennie at that time was all dazzle, leather jacket and blonde hair, and was the darling of the newspapers, top scorer in the country, dating a page three model – it was a boom time for him and for West Ham.

Collecting newspaper headlines inspired my early morning paper round, and my granddad's house at the halfway point was the place where I would study the back pages of the tabloids for the latest transfer gossip (with a cup of tea and half a pack of Marks and Spencer's finger creams). We finished that season in a best-ever third place, narrowly behind title-winning Liverpool and losing second place to Everton in the final game of the season. Despite the unprecedented success, West Ham's average home league attendance was 21,179 and football had yet to go through its Italia 90 renaissance.

Coming from 'posh London' in Hampstead, my dad prefers rugby, having enjoyed a healthy junior career with a different-shaped ball. But the first time I really understood that I was a West Ham fan was when I asked him and my mum for a shirt. While they have always supported me, I'm not sure they understood what it meant to support West Ham, and one Saturday they returned from Rathbone Street Market in Canning Town with a kit as a gift: a yellow kit. A Watford kit. In a box.

They thought I would be grateful. Everyone else was wearing claret and blue, so this would help me to stand out in the park – like Banana Man in a convent. If I remember rightly, Umbro were selling kits in a box as one of those new fads, and my parents thought that (a) it was cheaper than other kits; (b) it was a complete kit rather than just a shirt; (c) it looked very tidy in a box; and (d) it was bright (yellow shirts, red shorts, Iveco sponsors – I don't recall the colour of the socks because I never got that far before throwing a rather large tantrum).

This was before the age when every playground or training pitch has a Lionel Messi or Cristiano Ronaldo shirt. You were born local and supported local. No arguments. When I went to Brampton Manor secondary school up the road from the stadium, we had one Liverpool fan in the team and everyone else was West Ham. I don't remember ever seeing anyone wearing a Watford strip (unless they wore it indoors).

It has always been West Ham for me. Win or lose. There is something about the way they play, the players they have, the hope (and despair). 'Just like my dreams they fade and die' from 'Bubbles' sums it up: nobody supports West Ham for the glory.

All this was represented in that final game at Upton Park against Manchester United: the claustrophobic atmosphere before the game; the need to beat them after losing 2–1 in the FA Cup sixth round replay, just one darn game from Wembley; the final crescendo on our home turf which had been the venue for so many stories. How many other teams can claim an 8–1 win with a hat-trick from the centre half against three different goalkeepers? If you're a true West Ham fan you don't need reminding it was Alvin Martin against Newcastle (the keepers: Martin Thomas, defender Chris Hedworth, striker Peter Beardsley).

If that 1986 match was high drama, the final fixture at the stadium was something else altogether: leading 1–0, trailing 2–1... then winning 3–2 against Manchester United with a late goal from defender Winston Reid. The match encapsulated what supporting West Ham means. We never make it easy – we always do it the hard way. Those images are captured in this book.

Supporting West Ham has meant joyously appreciating Sir Trevor Brooking, Billy Bonds, Bobby Moore, Sir Geoff Hurst, Ray Stewart, Alvin Martin – and now Dimitri Payet, that wonderful, gifted French international from the island of Réunion. It has also meant understanding the queue that stretched 200-plus deep along the Barking Road from Nathan's Pies and Eels shop less than an hour before kickoff. There have been stands and statues, songs and memories. There has been joy and heartbreak and, as the Club moves to the sparkling Olympic Stadium, none of us who have followed West Ham will forget what has happened before.

Over many days in that final, dramatic season my *Daily Mail* colleague and award-winning photographer Andy Hooper captured images of players, legends and supporters, iconic images of a stadium that had been 'home' since 1904. We had 15,000 images to edit and we selected our favourites for the following pages.

Together, in association with West Ham, we have compiled this picture book to commemorate the farewell to Upton Park, including many behind-the-scenes images and access-all-areas photographs. I wonder what your favourite will be?

'Great grazing' as we like to call it – it is a book of few words, but many images. We hope all West Ham supporters will cherish it as a reminder of more than a hundred years of occupying the same ground before moving to a deluxe new home. Yes, it is farewell, but this book means these memories will stay forever. I hope you enjoy looking through it as much as we enjoyed pulling it together.

Personally, I would like to thank my partner, Kate, for the sunshine she has brought to my life and to my mum and dad. I forgive you for the Watford kit. I would also like to mention my long-time friend and fellow West Ham season ticket holder Tony Moore for always arriving early with me before a game and for helping to inspire the idea behind this book. I love watching football with him.

See you all at the Olympic Stadium.

STANFORD-LE-HOPE
WORTHING
HAMMERS

THE FANS

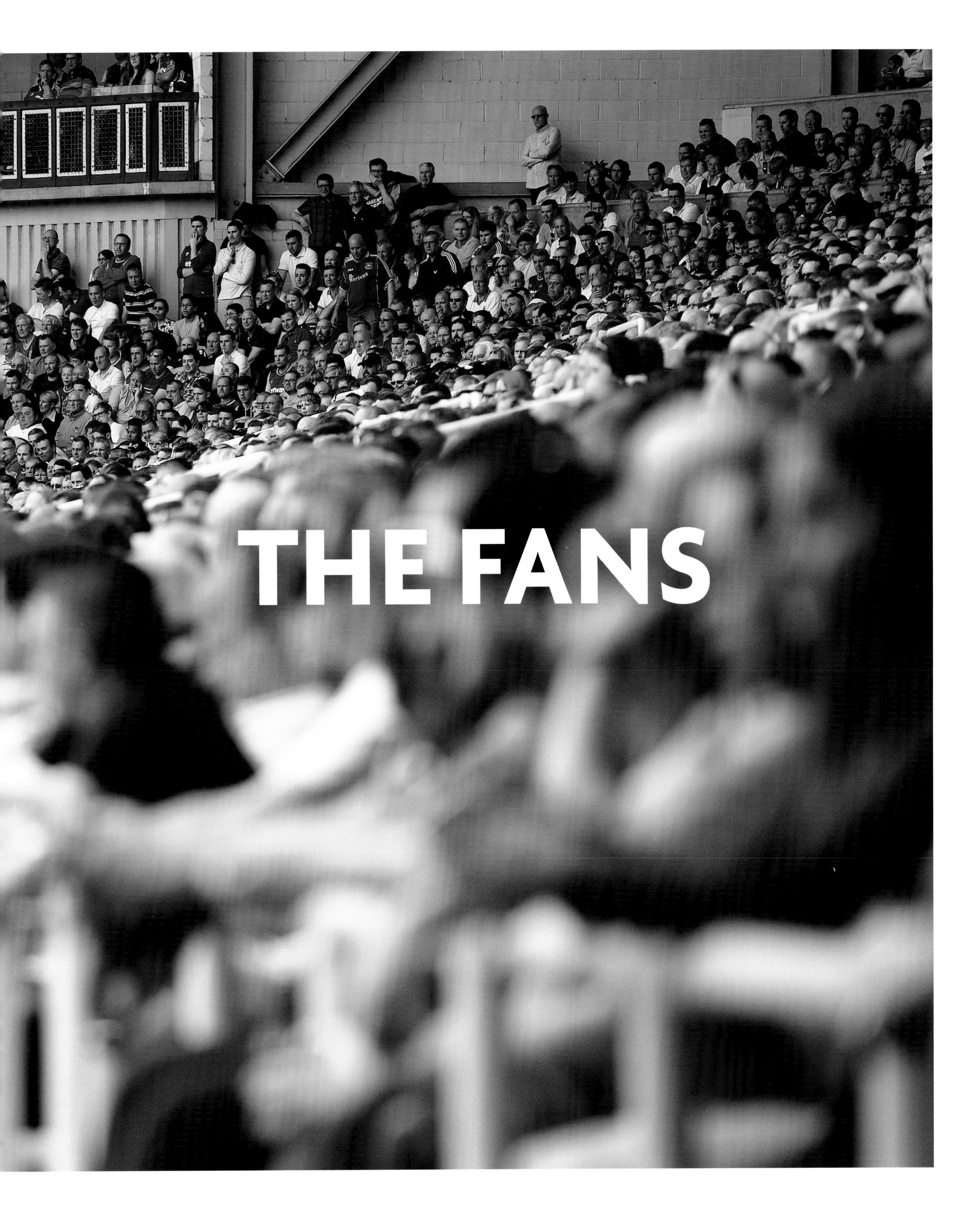

Autograph hunters strain to attract the attention of their heroes arriving in the players' car park. One programme already seems to have nine names signed on the back – the sign of a good afternoon's work.

MARK NOBLE
TEAMS
MARK
betway

Fans gather outside The Boleyn pub, on the junction of the Barking Road and Green Street, before the Swansea game in May. It's the last Saturday game at Upton Park.

THE BOLEYN
THE BOLEYN
Controlled
ZONE
Mon - Sat
8 am - 6.30 pm
330
Canning Town
betwa
WEST HAM

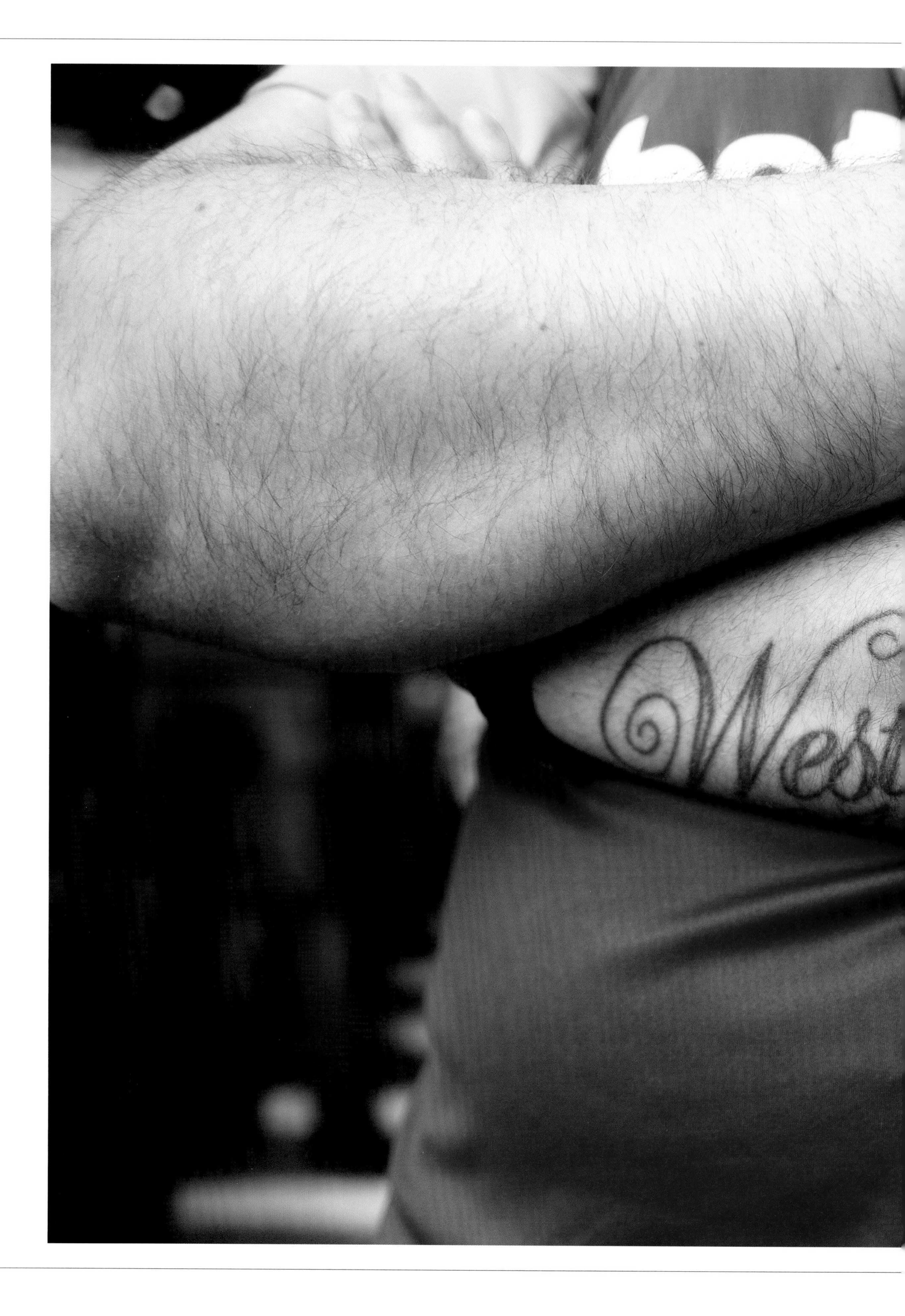

WEST HAM SINGH
28

Four images that sum up what it can be like to follow West Ham: from the hope of an opportunity created to the despair of an opportunity scorned. We keep coming back for more though.

umbro
betway
adidas
alpari

betway
adidas

Strangers embrace. Leaving the ground that you've visited your whole life is one of those 'we're never going to be here again' moments.

WE ARE
MACMILLAN.
CANCER SUPPORT
100+

etw

CATERPILLAR
GROUND
CLEARANCE

adidas

A young fan clasps her hands together anxiously, hoping for a celebration to follow.

Locked out, but with something to shout about. These fans climb the walls in Priory Road to make their voices heard on match day. Upton Park was 99.8 per cent full in its final season, as West Ham filled its ground more than any other Premier League club.

WEST HAM UNITED
FAREWELL BOLEYN
1904 - 2016
EXIT
Gangway keep clear

Losing to Swansea, so the supporters in the Bobby Moore Stand stay below decks and enjoy the party atmosphere instead – there was a song or two about Spurs failing to win the league too.

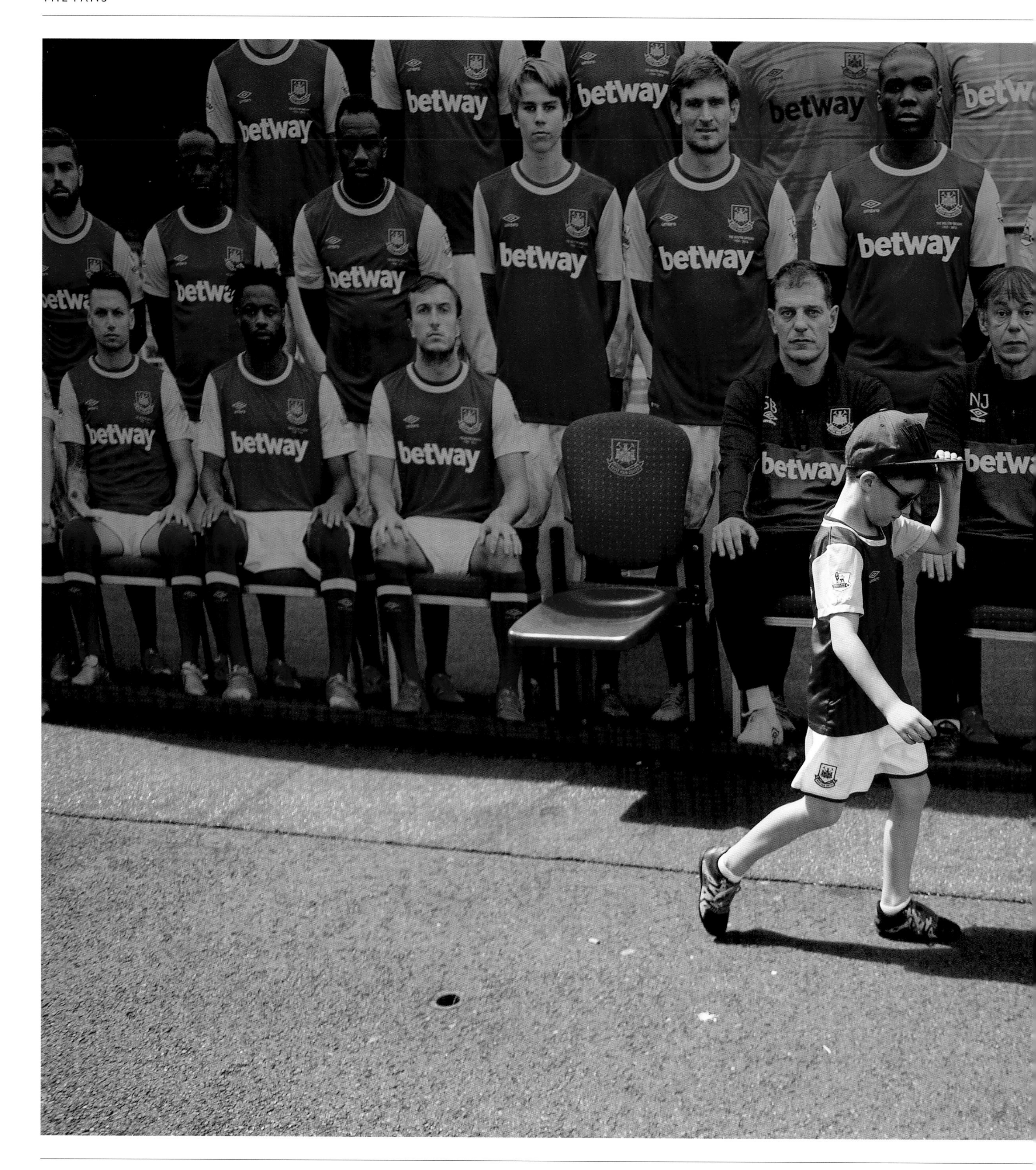
betway
betway
betway
betway
betway
betway
betway
betway
betway
betway
SB
NJ

Have your picture taken with the team? This young fan appears to doff his cap as he strolls past.

SALES LTD
BED SHOP
SALE
SALE

GREEN STREET
THE BOLEYN
7am - 8pm
No loading
7am - 8pm
SORRY
NO
AWAY
SUPPORTERS

Avalanche

Taking a quiet moment on Castle Street at half time in a game against Watford.

Smartphones at half time: hopelessly looking for a reception on their mobiles. Fingers crossed for a better connection at the Olympic Stadium!

What's it all about Alfie? A young supporter hitches a lift for a better view.

Ready for battle: it could be a bit lively around Upton Park, but are the suits of armour really necessary chaps?

A shirt that has seen a few games... This Sixties away shirt is synonymous with Bobby Moore's time at the Club.

West Ham boys are a
little bit stronger

PRIVATE
FUNCTIONS
&
SPECIAL
EVENTS
NOW CATERED FOR
CONTACT US FOR MORE INFO.
WEST HAM F.C
AS YOU ALL KNOW, WEST HAM ARE MOVING TO THE OLYMPIC PARK, STRATFORD FOR THE 2016/17 SEASON. WE WANT TO KEEP THE SPIRIT OF THE BOLEYN PUB GOING, SO WE ARE OFFERING AN ANNUAL MEMBERSHIP THAT WILL PROVIDE TRANSPORT FROM THE BOLEYN TO STRATFORD FOR EVERY HOME GAME.
£120
PER YEAR.
ENTERTAINMENT
PUB
QUIZ?
THURSDAY 26 MAY
@8pm
TICKETS AVAILABLE
FROM THE BAR!
LATE NIGHT
WEST HAM UNITED
alpari
FX TRADING

BOLEYN THROUGH THE AGES

West Ham vs Reading at Upton Park in 1914 (*previous pages*).

Not sure what today's health and safety officers would say about this! Fans take a view of Upton Park from the flats next door during the 1972 FA Cup replay against Hereford, with supporters on the roof and leaning over the balconies.

Manchester United won the title on this day in 1967, but on this occasion West Ham reserve goalkeeper Colin Mackleworth, who played only three league games for the Club, foils Denis Law. West Ham eventually lost the match 6-1.

The crowd in 1933.

Alan Devonshire, a wonderfully gifted left winger who the Club signed for £5,000 from Southall, lifts the FA Cup on the balcony of Newham Town Hall in May 1980. The Denmark Arms across the road offered some light refreshment for the West Ham fans gathered below.

Before the days of training grounds, snow meant West Ham players could not train on the pitch, so they cleared the car park and wore plimsolls instead, as seen at this session in 1964.

He always had time on the ball and here Bobby Moore uses a break in play to take a breather in a 1973 0-0 draw with Derby County.

Carlos Tevez, who is revered by West Ham supporters for his impact on the team during the 2006–07 season, celebrates a goal in front of his appreciative audience.

Taken by *Newham Recorder* photographer Steve Bacon in 1980, this photograph epitomises Billy Bonds. Bonds had been clattered in a match and sustained head injuries, but it was only when the film was later processed that the photographer realised the legendary West Ham captain still had blood trickling down his nose as he posed for the photograph before driving home to his family in Kent.

West Ham 5, Castilla 1 (September 1980). A European victory played behind closed doors, with supporters banned after violence in the first leg in Madrid. The game had an official crowd of 262, mainly police and journalists – West Ham's lowest ever attendance. David Cross scored a hat-trick, the only player to do so in European competition for the Club.

It looks like a building site! With work taking place in 2001 on the main stand, Alan Shearer and Robert Lee are out first for Newcastle United and Paolo Di Canio leads out West Ham.

Master penalty-taker Ray Stewart celebrates with (from left to right) Frank Lampard Sr, Trevor Brooking and Stuart Pearson after scoring the late winner against Aston Villa in the 1980 FA Cup run.

Bobby Moore shows off the trophy to supporters after the 1964 success against Preston.

It wasn't the White Horse final, but a fine stallion leads the FA Cup winners' bus parade in 1975.

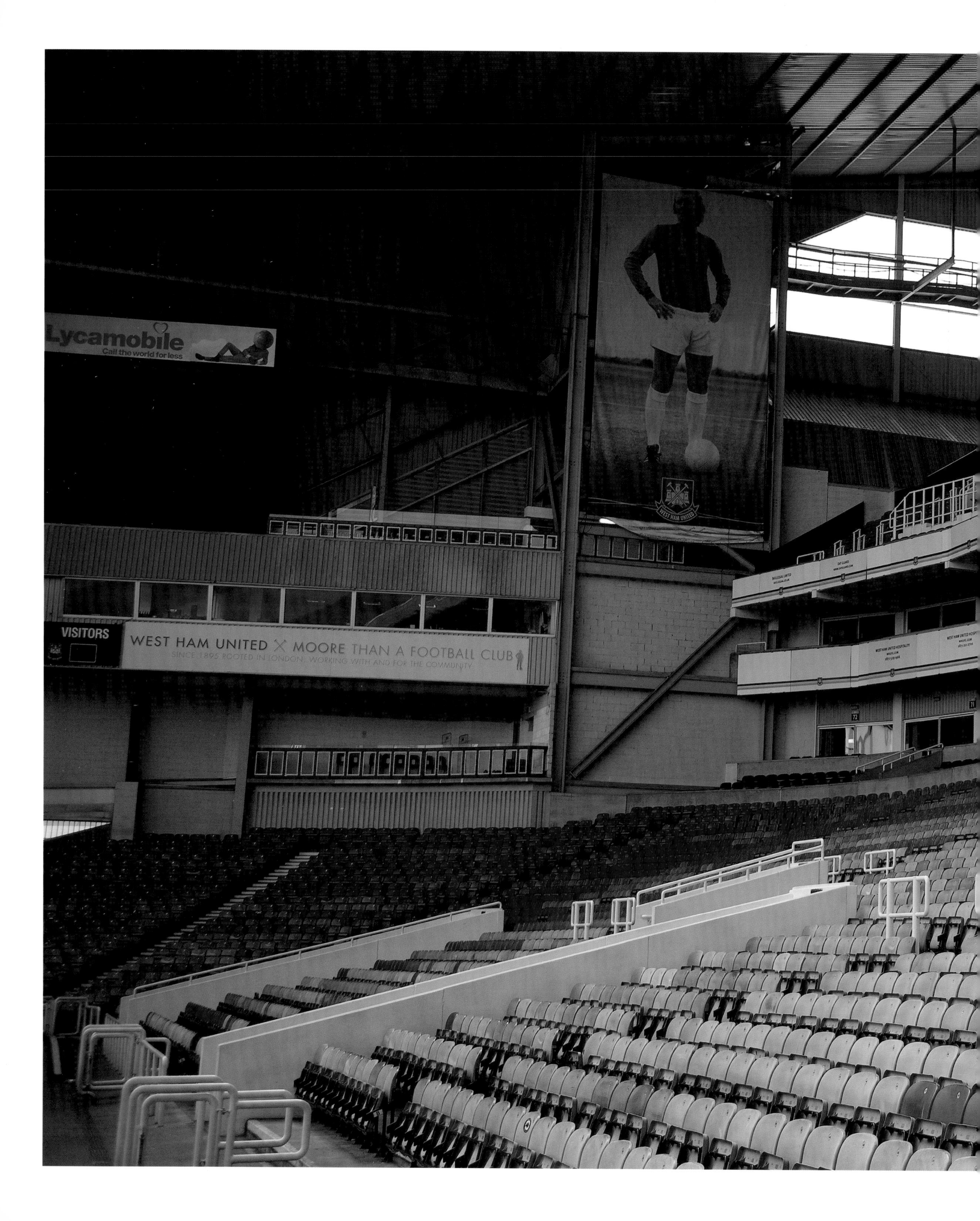
Lycamobile
Call the world for less
VISITORS
WEST HAM UNITED MOORE THAN A FOOTBALL CLUB
SINCE 1895 ROOTED IN LONDON. WORKING WITH AND FOR THE COMMUNITY

OUR HOME

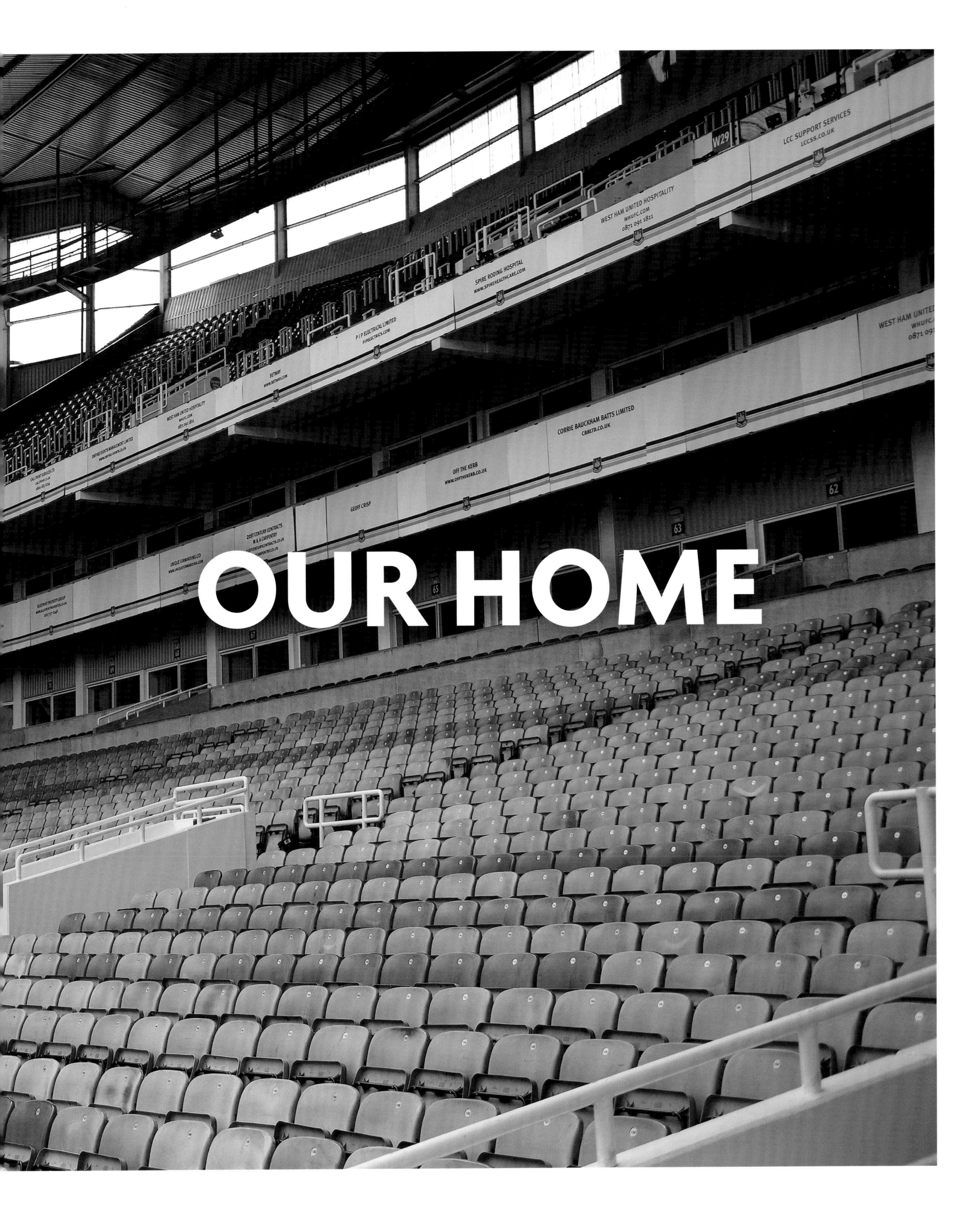
LCC SUPPORT SERVICES
LCCSS.CO.UK
W29
WEST HAM UNITED HOSPITALITY
WHUFC.COM
0871 091 1811
SPIRE RODING HOSPITAL
WWW.SPIREHEALTHCARE.COM
CORRIE BAUCKHAM BATTS LIMITED
CBBLTD.CO.UK
OFF THE KERB
WWW.OFFTHEKERB.CO.UK
GEOFF CRISP
62
63
65

betway
THE ACADE
OF
FOOTBAL

umbro
FOUNDED
IN
1895
WEST HAM UNITED

SEATS 90 to 150
SEATS 90 to 150

WEST HAM UNITED

Tranquility while the match-day build-up pulsates outside. Sister Immaculata and Sister Patricia preside at the Our Lady of Compassion church in the shadow of the main stand (*see left*).

betway
WEST HAM UNITED
betway

The Kit Room at Upton Park. A drawer for each player (*above*) and two shirts for every game for each player (*below*). The shirts pictured are for the final match against Manchester United.

RESERVED FOR
CHAIRMAN

FAREWELL BOLEYN
1904 - 2016
JOIN US ON
OUR GREATEST
JOURNEY YET
SEASON TICKETS
2016/17
Adults from £289
Kids just £99
JOIN THE PRIORITY LIST
reservations.whufc.com
25

The players' entrance to the dressing room area, with a board signed by each player to commemorate the final season.

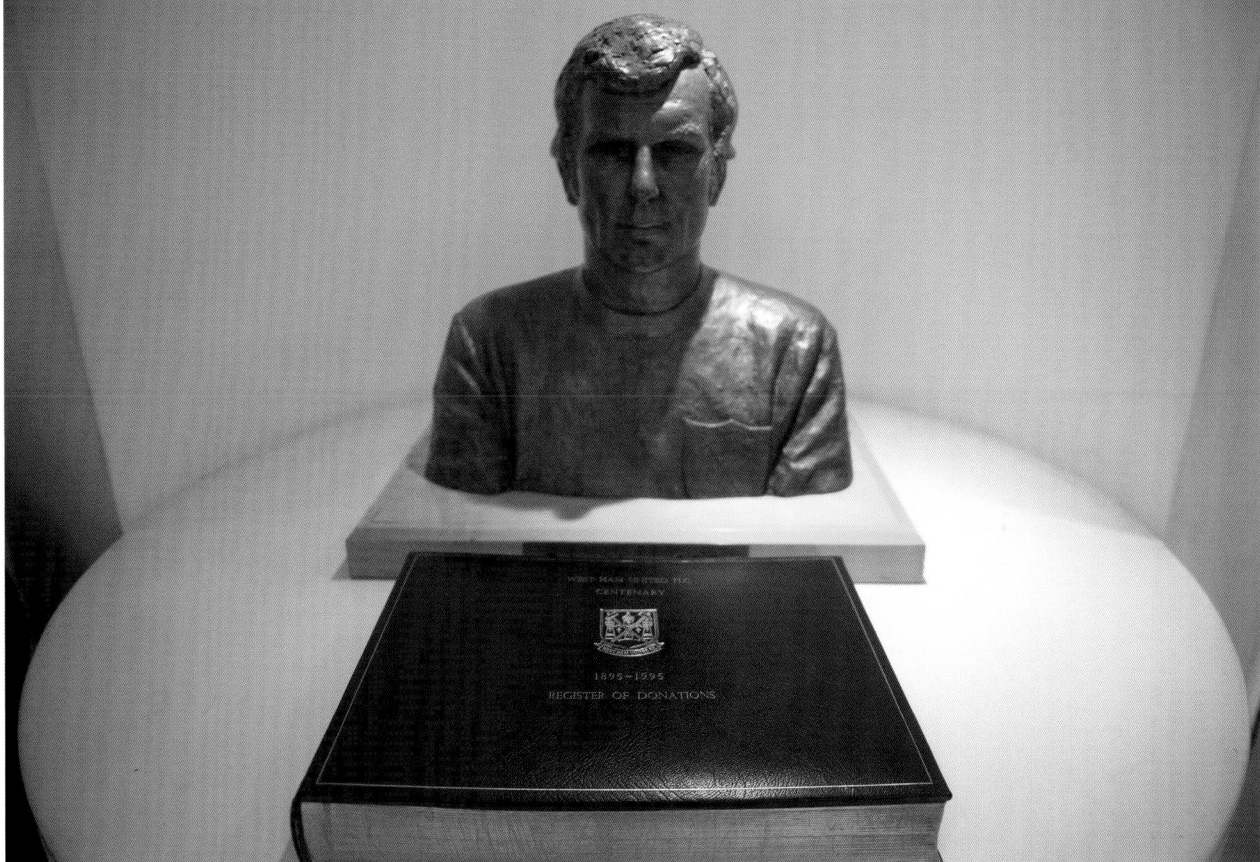

A bust of Bobby Moore at the entrance to the Bobby Moore Stand along with a 'register of donations' book to commemorate West Ham's centenary year in 1995.

Commemorative bricks: the Club has promised to move all of the messages to Champions Place in the Olympic Park.

29

betway
PLEASE
KEEP OFF
THE GRASS

betway
betway
betway
betway
betway
betway
betway
betway
betway
betway
betway
betway
betway
betway

HOME DRESSING ROOM
NO
UNAUTHORISED
PERSONNEL ALLOWED
IN DRESSING ROOM
ONLY
COACHING STAFF
& MEDICAL

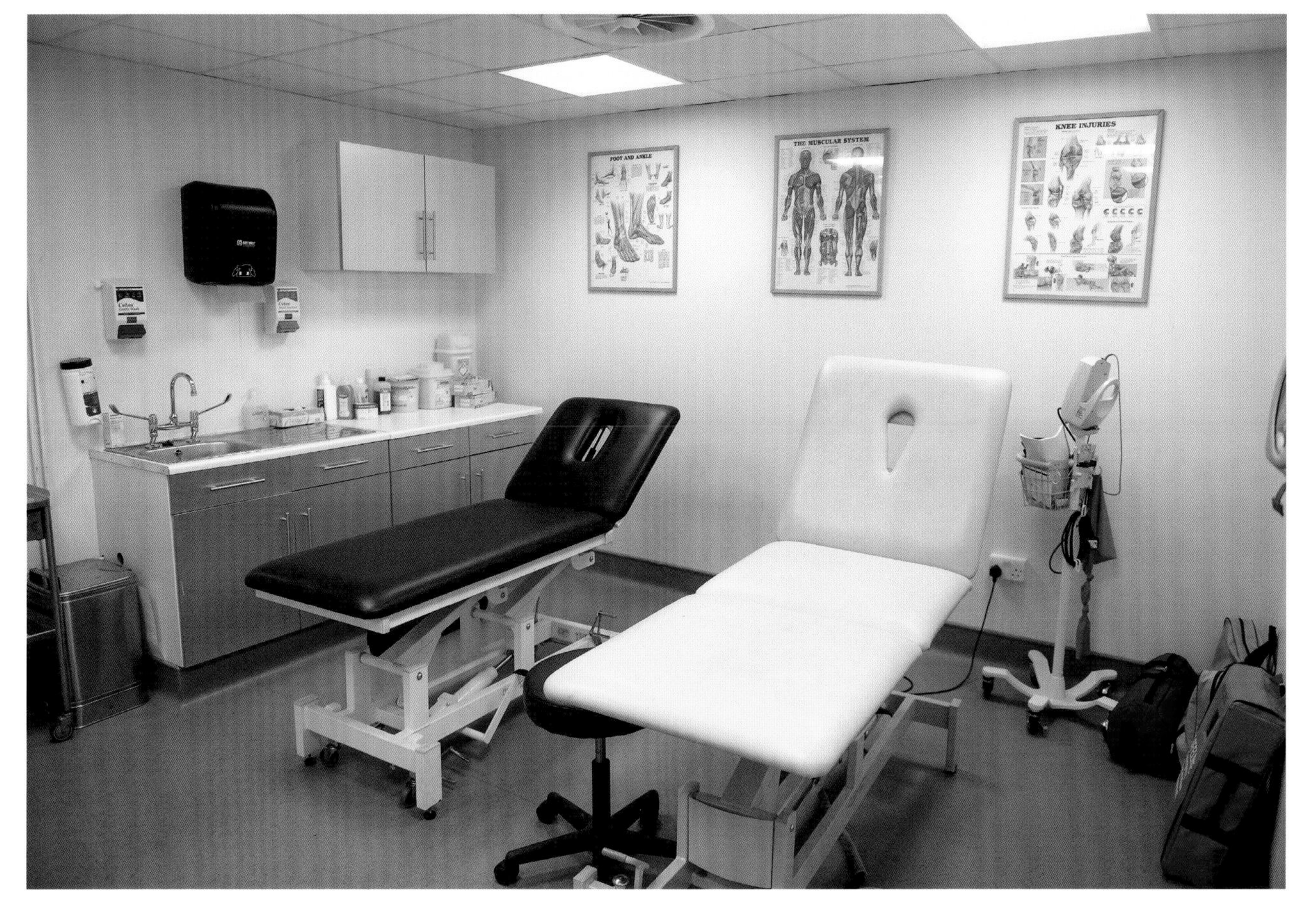

The home team dressing room, showers and medical room.

EAST STAND TURNSTILES
68
69

CLIC Sargent
for children with cancer
CLIC Sargent
for children with cancer
Help us support children and young people with cancer

THAN A KING
PRAWN IN A
COCKTAIL
DRESS

BELLY BUSTERS

A stall of club memorabilia takes up the parking space of this property in Green Street. This is the night the lights went out on Liverpool in the FA Cup with West Ham defender Angelo Ogbonna scoring in the 120th minute.

LIVERPOOL
W.HAM
LIVERPOOL
PROPER
EAST
COYI
I WAS
THERE
THIS IS AN
WEST
WEST
WEST
Mon - Sat
8am - 6.30pm

WEST HAM UNITED
WEST HAM UNITED
WEST HAM UNITED

Gary Firmanger, editor of the *Over Land and Sea* fanzine and one of the regular and more popular figures around Upton Park.

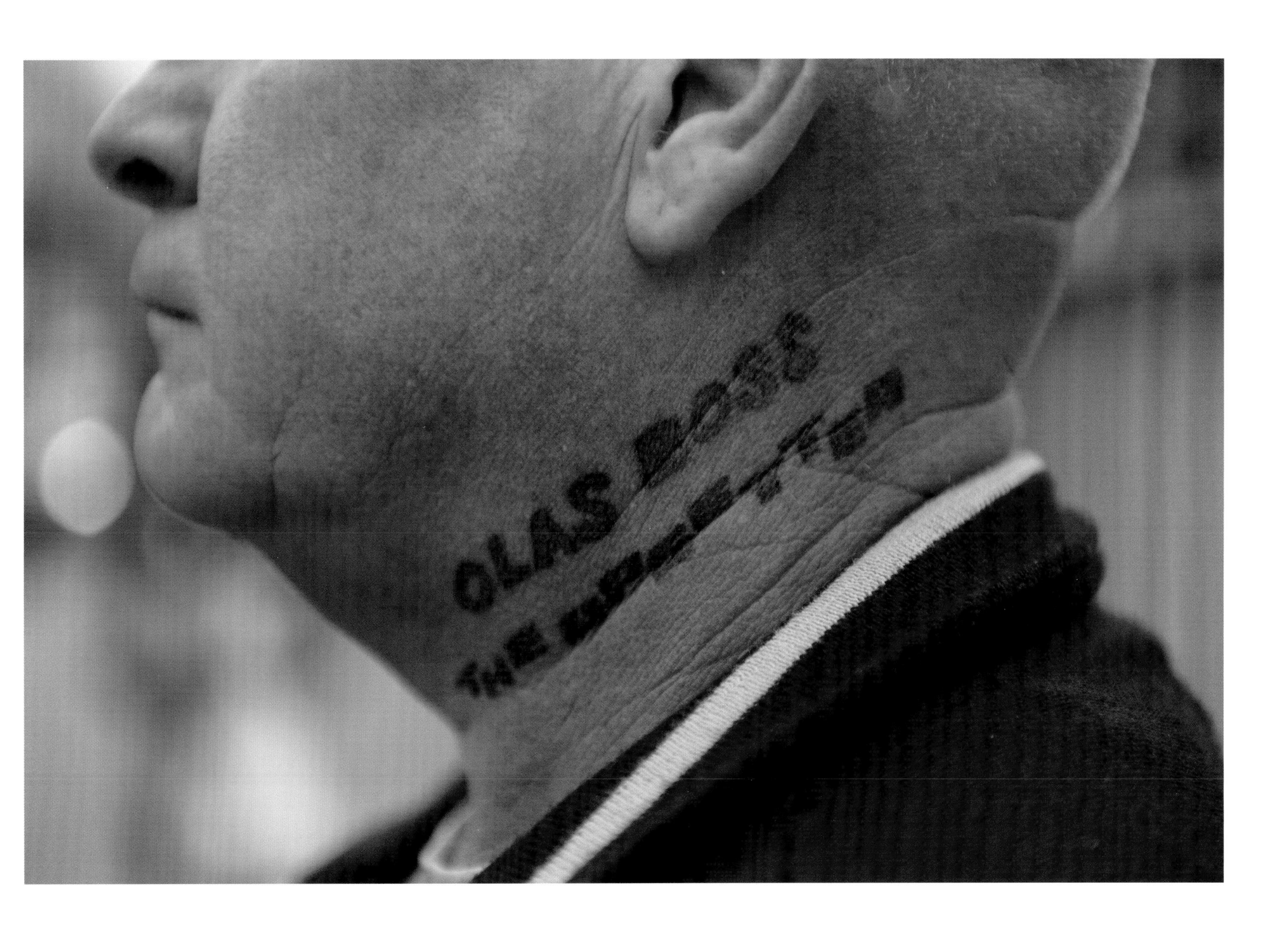

Best view in the house. Mark Gardner at his mum's property with his son, Reece, in the flats overlooking the ground. Fans used to knock and offer to pay £10 to share the view. Have there been many better views in football?

REEC
11

Looking cool in the queue for pie and mash at Nathan's.

Collecting subs in the Supporters' Club in Castle Street.

Bobby Moore would run through brick walls for West Ham. This artist's impression can be found in Green Street.

38
CARD
HOLDERS
ONLY
betway
STAND
LOWER TIER
39
CARD
HOLDERS
ONLY

TICKETS
HERE

39
CARD
HOLDERS
ONLY
15
PLEASE DO NOT
PARK IN FRONT
OF THESE GATES
IN CONSTANT USE
MAX HEIGHT

Inside a match is taking place, but outside this lady is walking her dog (and taking a sneaky view) through the gates used by the ambulance service. The dog seems more interested in Andy Hooper and his cameras.

BARKING RD E6

Sending out a message on behalf of the West Ham Foundation, which has celebrated 25 years of work in the community in East London and Essex.

In the shadow of Upton Park, supporters take a drink and a share a smile in The Boleyn pub a few hours before the rush towards kick off.

Inside the West Ham Supporters' Club in Castle Street.

Stickers from clubs all around Europe cover the sign for the Sir Trevor Brooking Stand. I wonder which sticker was there first?

A kick-about before kick off.

ORE STAND LOWER TIER SEATING
43
CARD HOLDER ONLY
44
CARD HOLDERS ONLY
45
CARD HOLDERS ONLY
YOU ARE LIABLE TO BE
SEARCHED
AS A CONDITION OF ENTRY
16

STOP LOOKING
AT MY
ARSE!
ORDER A
DRINK
AND ASK US
ABOUT OUR

A view south from Upton Park. In the background, the Excel Exhibition Centre, in Royal Victoria Dock, looks like another football stadium.

David Gold, the Club's Co-chairman, used to live at 442 Green Street, now 'Ceejays', a hair and beauty centre. The current owners are happy to allow David to take a look inside. How many other club owners in the Premier League used to live opposite the stadium that they owned?

Co-chairmen, sharp rollers.

1904-2016
112
YEARS
The Boleyn Ground
WEST HAM UNITED F.C.
YOUTH ACADEMY
THE ACADEMY
EAST LONDON
DUBLIN HAMMERS
WEST HAM UNITED SUPPORTERS
WEST HAM UTD

Inside the Supporters' Club.

The never-ending queue for pie and mash at Nathan's on match day, and plenty of smiles inside.

Relaxing in The Boleyn before kick off.

The walk from Upton Park station to the Boleyn Ground took supporters past Queen's Market, which opened in 1904, the same year that the Club moved in.

MATCH DAY

umbro
betway
umbro

POLICE HORSES
CEI

In one of the cramped and stuffy interview rooms, Michail Antonio takes a call as he is about to be interviewed by the media.

Manager Slaven Bilić's private room, where he would entertain friends, colleagues and guests after a match. Ironically, this image captures former West Ham captain Billy Bonds on the TV screen. There is an artist's impression of the Olympic Stadium on the wall (left).

Dimitri Payet described Slaven Bilić as 'my father' after winning the Player of the Year Award, following a stunning debut season in the Premier League. Here, their shirts are side by side in the dressing room before Mark Noble's testimonial. The message alongside is clear.

WEST HAM UNITED
WINNING
ITS
WHAT
WE ARE
HERE FOR

Payet preparing for action before a Premier League game. He scored nine league goals in his first season with the Club.

James Tomkins, Joey O'Brien and Aaron Cresswell at the mouth of the tunnel waiting to go out onto the pitch.

A sneaky puff during a match for this steward.

Legendary defender Julian Dicks, who joined Slaven Bilić's backroom team in 2015, keeps a watchful eye on proceedings.

Manager Slaven Bilić prowls the touchline as Dimitri Payet accelerates into space. In response, the Watford defence appear to scatter.

betway
betway
14
CATHCART
15

Popular captain Mark Noble prepares to take a corner and is greeted in typical fashion by the fans.

Plenty of bottle: as with all the stadia in English football, alcohol cannot be consumed in view of the playing surface, so there is much is left behind as fans return to their seats after half time.

Look, no hands: James Collins and his daughter enjoy some time together before the action begins.

Typical of the work that goes on during a game: programme sellers' takings are counted in a portacabin.

Tea Lady 'Auntie Lesley': 33 years at the Club, in her kitchen just off the players' tunnel. She takes care of the players and press (and her favourite player was Teddy Sheringham).

The match day catering staff limber up for their duties.

The BBC's Dan Walker watches Manchester United and England captain Wayne Rooney report for action in the away team dressing room.

The line-up is on the board and Andy Carroll is taking photos of his team-mates.

Slaven Bilić wants West Ham to push forward and 'press the play' (against Swansea).

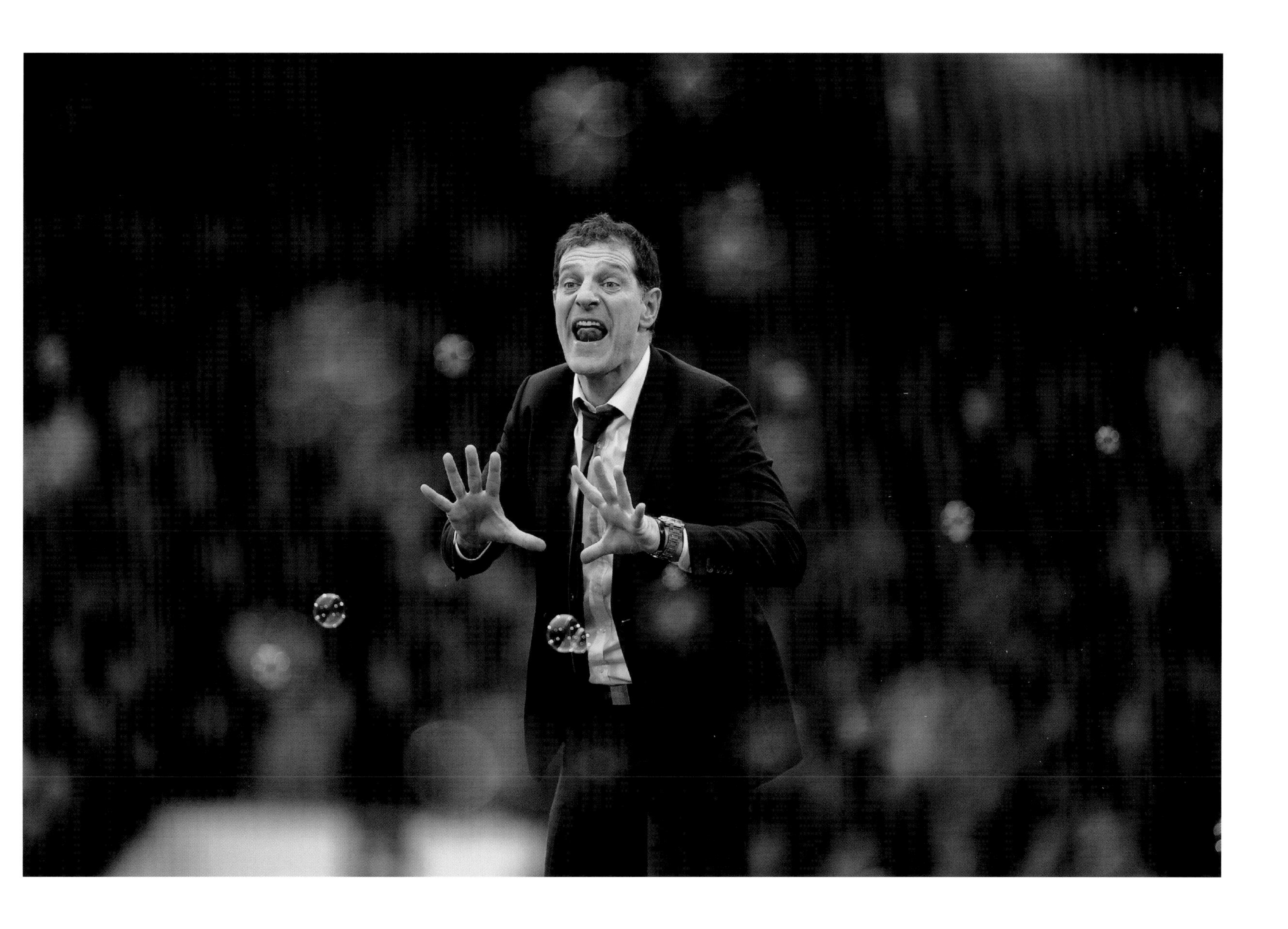

CRESSWELL
3

Mark Noble and his team-mates see the funny side of a message left in his locker.

Diafra Sakho keeps a beady eye on Andy Hooper, who has been allowed special access to the private dressing rooms.

Goalkeeper Adrián throws up his bib from the tunnel.

Night games were always popular at Upton Park for the atmosphere under the lights, but this club official (*see below*) appears to be looking to the heavens before returning to his post.

Payet tries to find a way through
two Swansea markers.

Michail Antonio trudges off after the final whistle. West Ham lost 4-1 in their final Saturday match at Upton Park.

betway
betway
betwa
WEST HAM UNITED
16
umbro

betway

KICK IT OUT

Payet's devilish set plays caused chaos in opposition defences. Andy Carroll, moving in from the edge of the penalty area, is the target for this delivery.

Co-chairman David Gold and Club Solicitor Henri Brandman escort a supporter and his companion before kick off.

Co-chairman David Sullivan leaves in the rain and pauses to speak to supporters.

The Champions statue, with Bobby Moore held aloft by Sir Geoff Hurst, Martin Peters and Ray Wilson (Everton). A supporter has placed a claret and blue scarf around his neck. The statue, which cost £725,000 and was sculpted by Philip Jackson, will move with West Ham. The Club contributed some of the money to the statue, which was erected in 2003.

The match commander and his pre-match briefing where he addresses safety and fan control with the match and club officials. *Insert:* New technology at the old stadium; digital watches which inform the officials if a ball has bounced over the goal-line.

2 March 2016: Captain Mark Noble leads out the team for the last match against Spurs at Upton Park. West Ham won 1-0 to damage Tottenham's chances of success. Michail Antonio scored the winning goal – it was a great night!

ADRIAN
13
betway

Mercedes-Benz
clarkes

Co-chairman David Gold addresses goalkeeper Darren Randolph before a league match.

MOORE

THE LEGENDS OF UPTON PARK

Billy Bonds is all smiles after a visit to the stadium. Bonds played 799 games for the Club, his last was aged 41 years and 225 days.

Two superstars: Sir Trevor Brooking and actor and West Ham supporter Ray Winston, who is at the ground filming a documentary.

Teddy Sheringham and young fans before the England vs Germany 'Legends' match 50 years after England won the World Cup.

betway betway betway betway

PLEASE
KEEP OFF
THE GRASS

In safe hands: Club Chaplain Alan Bolding in the players' lounge with Tony Carr, a man responsible for so many young players being developed by the Club.

Warm greetings, old friends: Paolo Di Canio and Luděk Mikloško.

The away dressing room for Mark Noble's testimonial. Craig Bellamy holds court (*above*) and Chris Powell and Luděk Miklośko are thrilled to catch up (*below*).

WEST HAM UNITED
umbro
betway
umbro

Di Canio responds to the pleas of supporters to sign autographs.

Bobby Zamora, who scored West Ham's winning goal in the play-off final against Preston in 2005, talks with Slaven Bilić.

Everyone – even Rio Ferdinand – checks out the team sheet to see if they have been selected.

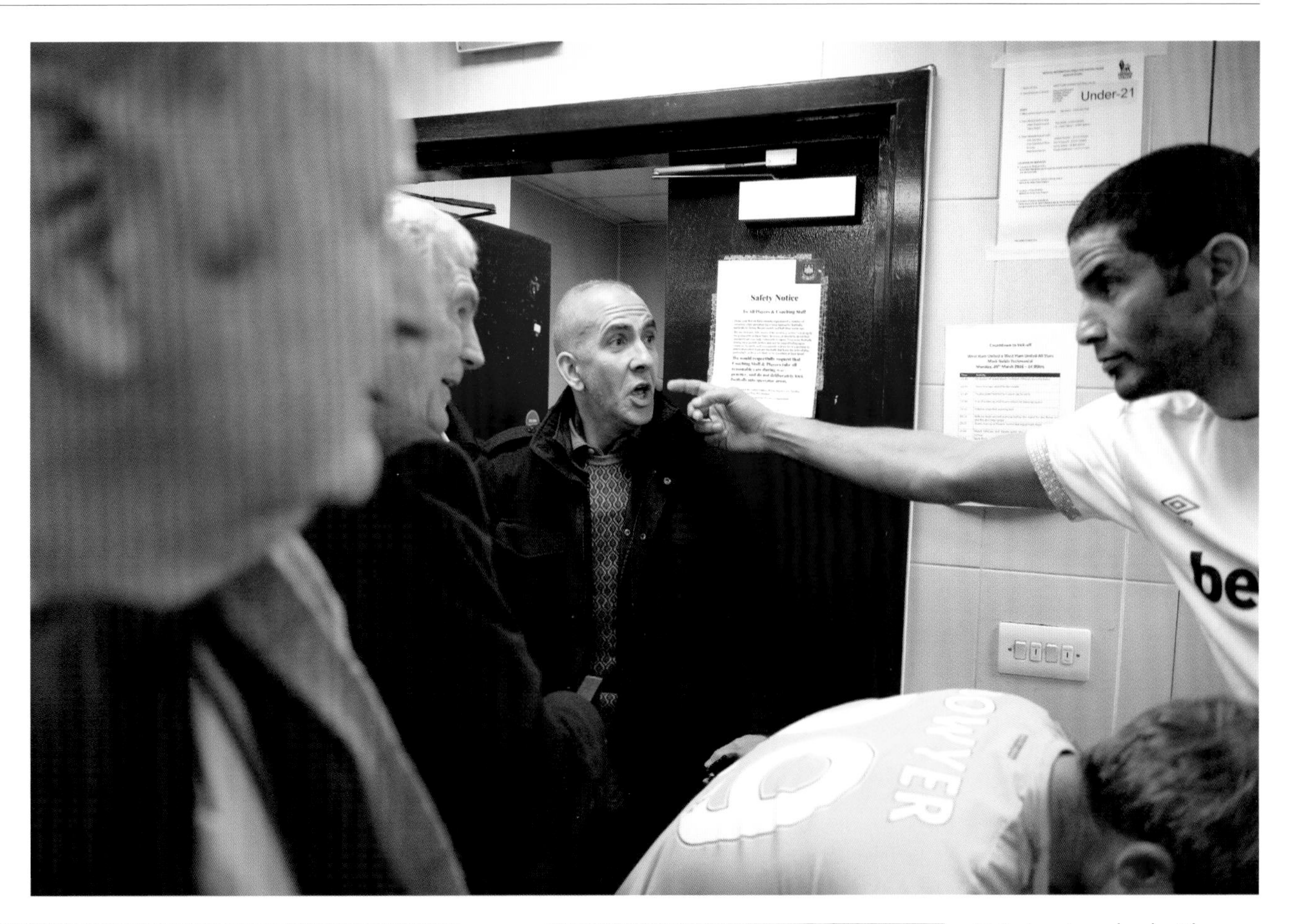

Di Canio enjoys a laugh with former team-mates David James (*above*) and Chris Powell (*left*).

It's not Pat Cash at Wimbledon! A smiling Chris Powell leaps over the advertising boards and ends up running into the Sir Trevor Brooking Stand.

STEWART
2
DICKS
3
BONDS
4
MARTIN
5
PETERS
7
HURST
9
BROOKING
8
DI CANIO
10
11
6

Trevor Sinclair is happy to be back at his old stomping ground.

David James warms up.

Homeland actor Damian Lewis joins David Haye and other celebrities for the England vs Germany 'Legends' game.

Never say goodbye,
Because goodbye
Means going away,
And going away
Means forgetting.
Thanks for the Memories
Upton Park. Farewell Boleyn
Love from Jonjo

THE FINAL GAME

KEPT
WEST HAM

BE
OCKED
ITED
ERS CLUB
MEMBERS ENTRANCE
Members Only
COFFEE

Former Head of Communications Paul Stringer briefs Co-chairman David Gold.

It's the home team dressing room and Manchester United are delayed in heavy traffic, so the pre-match preparations have to be changed. The game kicks off 45 minutes late.

It's a long way up! Jamie Redknapp climbs towards the TV gantry. Sky covered the game live.

A special edition of the *Evening Standard* for the last game at the Upton Park ground.

The Manchester United bus arrives. The team came needing a win in order to continue their chances of qualifying for the Champions League.

A graffiti message (claret wall, blue paint).

The Romford Drum and Trumpet Corps played 'Abide With Me' as part of the pre-match ceremony. Images later flashed up on the giant screens of former players and managers who have sadly passed away, including Ron Greenwood, John Lyall, John Bond and Dylan Tombides, bringing tears to the eyes of many inside the stadium.

10 May 2016: West Ham vs Manchester United. The teams come out for the last time...

betway

A semi fish-eye lens captures the kick off; the Hammers' crest shines out from one of the big screens, newly installed for the final game.

One supporter shares his views with Manchester United fans.

Joy in the Bobby Moore Stand as
West Ham score.

View from the back of the lower tier of the Sir Trevor Brooking Stand as Manchester United attempt to clear their lines.

BOLEYN
GAME
No.2398
WEST HAM UNITED
V
MANCHESTER UNITED
TUESDAY 10 MAY 2016

As tempers fray, Manchester United manager Louis Van Gaal is confronted by James Collins, one of West Ham's substitutes, nicknamed the 'Ginger Pelé'.

betway

Great Memories
Great Friends
WHUFC

FAREWELL TO THE BOLEYN GROUND
PTON
PAR
112 YEARS OF HISTORY, PRIDE & PASSION
1904 -
FINAL TIME
FAREWELL BOLEYN

West Ham lead 1-0 and goal-scorer Diafra Sakho is joined by celebrating team-mates.

West Ham are ahead and the supporters are in full voice.

Pay As You Go SIM
national & international
betway
betway
betway
betway

The final goal at Upton Park. Defender Winston Reid reacts first to a Dimitri Payet cross to tower above the Manchester United defence. He beats Daley Blind (*above*) ... Then his header is too strong for goalkeeper David de Gea (*right*) ... Then he runs off to celebrate. Look at the faces of joy on West Ham's players (*far right*) ... and despair for Manchester United's defenders.

CHEVROLET
betway

Spot the ball? A typically frantic moment in a Premier League match. Chris Smalling has his hands in Andy Carroll's face as team-mates crowd in.

SMALLING
12
28
9

The match is over and an emotional Mark Noble and Andy Carroll salute the supporters.

betway

Carroll is photographed with girlfriend Billi and their son Arlo.

Dimitri Payet and his three sons take to the field at Upton Park for one last time. Each of the boys has a similar haircut to their dad.

The great Martin Peters is shielded from the rain in the farewell send-off.

The fireworks begin (*right*) and Mark Noble leads the players back out through the smoke for one last time to say 'thank you' (*above right*).

Slaven Bilić takes a moment during the farewell.

A view from outside the ground as the fireworks shoot into the night sky.

betway
WEST HAM UNITED
betway

The platform in the middle of the pitch as the players gather and captain Mark Noble is interviewed by Ben Shepherd. Bubbles the mascot looks on.

The players gather for one final picture in their dressing room before moving to the new facilities in Stratford. Cheikhou Kouyaté is in the middle making the crossed-arms 'Hammers' sign.

The last supper. After the game is over there is a selection of party food available for the players.

Co-chairman David Sullivan's boys, Jack and David, on the pitch.

ACKNOWLEDGEMENTS

We would like to thank West Ham, and in particular Karren Brady, for their support for this project and the access they provided. We understand that a Premier League football club dressing room is sacrosanct and that it is one place normally free from cameras. Andy Hooper, however, was allowed unique entry to private moments. We are grateful to West Ham for saying 'yes', more than they said 'no' to our requests.

Lee would also like to thank the team for their wonderful performances in the 2015–16 season which saw victories against Manchester City, Liverpool, Chelsea, Arsenal, Tottenham and, of course, Manchester United. It's hard to pick the best one (probably Spurs). It has been his favourite year for watching West Ham. In order, his best three players of the season are: Dimitri Payet, Mark Noble, Michail Antonio.

We would like thank the supporters – this is *their* book. We hope we have given you a book to be proud of and something you will want to keep and show your friends, family, children, grandchildren. There will never be another West Ham book like it (at least until they move out of the Olympic Stadium).

Also to Sophie Bradley, Joe Bookbinder and, especially, Paul Stringer in the West Ham press office for unlocking the doors and supporting our idea. To David Luxton for believing in the project and finding a publisher and to Trevor Davies, Pauline Bache and designer Jonathan Christie at Octopus Books for bringing the idea to life. We are thrilled.

Andy would like to thank his wife Lucy and children Calvin, Henry, Mary and Tommy for their support of the project. Andy says: 'I'm very lucky to have a career that I love but one that also takes me away from home more than I would like and I'm thankful they allow me to do that.'

Lee would like to thank his baby daughter Olive for finally getting some sleep, her big sister Molly for making him proud, and Kate for being amazing (and for letting him go to West Ham). 'I work long hours, but she gets what going to West Ham means to me,' Lee says. 'Now I just need to get her to marry me wearing claret and blue...'

Picture Credits

All pictures by Andy Hooper except for the following:
Action Images Frank Baron 62. **Alamy** Trinity Mirror/Mirrorpix 58 above. **Getty Images** Edward G. Malindine/ Topical Press Agency 56; Evening Standard 57 above; J. Wilds/Keystone 55; Norman Quicke/Express 63 above; Popperfoto 54, 60; Rolls Press/Popperfoto 63 below; Topical Press Agency 52. **Graham Hughes** 36 below left, 70 below left, 115 below right, 117, 147 above right, 186 above left, 187, 189, 216–7. **Offside** Mark Leech 61; Steve Bacon 59. **Press Association Images** Sean Dempsey/PA Archive 58 below. **Kevin Quigley** 206–7, 210–11, 215 below right. **REX Shutterstock** Twine/Daily Mail 57 below. **Ian Tuttle** 182–3, 191 above right, 192–3, 199, 203, 208–9, 212, 214 below left, 218